P9-CLD-349

BALD EAGLE

GORDON MORRISON

HOUGHTON MIFFLIN COMPANY BOSTON

1998

With love and affection this book is dedicated to my mother and father,
Hugh and Margaret, who raised ten nestlings of their own,
and to my wife, Nancy, for her love and dedication to our own three fledglings.

My sincere thanks to William Davis, eagle project leader,
Massachusetts Division of Fisheries and Wildlife, for generously sharing
his extensive knowledge and experience of bald eagles.

Walter Lorraine (wr) Books

Copyright © 1998 by Gordon Morrison

All rights reserved. For information about permission
to reproduce selections from this book, write to
Permissions, Houghton Mifflin Company, 215 Park
Avenue South, New York, New York 10003.

Library of Congress Cataloging-in-Publication Data

Morrison, Gordon.
    Bald eagle / written and illustrated by Gordon Morrison.
        p.   cm.
    ISBN 0–395–87328–2
    1. Bald eagle.   2. Bald eagle—Pictorial works.   I. Title.
QL696.F32M67   1998
598.9'43—dc21   97–42007
                                                      CIP

Printed in the United States of America

HOR   10   9   8   7   6   5   4   3   2   1

Today a baby bird
will hatch . . .
Using a hard bump on its beak
called an egg tooth, a baby bird
pushes against the inside
of its egg until it cracks.
Then, twisting and turning and
twisting and turning, the baby
bird pushes and cracks the egg
again and again.
After thirty-six hours of
pushing and cracking, it
finally breaks the egg
apart.
Lying among the
broken pieces is a
tired baby eagle.

1

Altricial and precocial — stages of development in different kinds of birds at hatching.

Altricial nestlings, like these robins, usually hatch naked, with closed eyes. They are helpless and totally dependent on their parents. Nests are usually in trees.

Precocial chicks, like these ruffed grouse, hatch covered in down, usually have their eyes open, and soon after move about and feed thcmselves. Nests are usually on the ground.

The semialtricial eaglets hatch covered in down, with their eyes closed, and are unable to move about. They depend on their parents for food and care. Nest is usually in trees.

In a day or two the other baby eagle hatches from its egg. Hatching is hard work. For the next few days the nestlings mostly rest and sleep. The mother and father eagles clean the broken eggshell from the nest and watch over their babies.

The mother and father eagles take
turns brooding, or sitting over the
nestlings to keep them warm and dry.
They also take turns feeding them.
Young birds need a lot to eat.

Nestling — a young, inactive
bird confined to nest.
Chick — a young,
usually active bird.
Eaglet — an eagle nestling.

Down — small soft
feathers formed to
conserve body heat.

Prenatal down is
developed in the egg.

Natal down replaces
prenatal down soon after
hatching and forms the base
for growing feathers.

Down in older birds is
covered by feathers.

Brood patch — an area of bare skin
under the feathers on an adult's
breast, where eggs are incubated
and nestlings are protected from heat,
cold, and rain.

4

In about a week the nestlings have grown bigger.
The soft white down they were born with is replaced by a coarser gray down, and their egg teeth fall off.

Egg tooth — a hard bump on the tip of the beak. All North American birds develop an egg tooth while in the egg. In some birds it falls off soon after hatching; in others it is absorbed. In eagles it falls off at 1 to 3 weeks.

Two weeks later the
nestlings are even bigger.
Feathers are starting to push through their
gray down. Their heads, feet, and beaks are
changing, and they are beginning to look more
like their mother and father. Once in a while
the baby birds try standing on their wobbly
legs, but they always fall into a downy heap.
They try again and again.

After only five weeks most of the
babies' down is covered by feathers.
The young birds are strong enough to stand
and begin to feed themselves. Soon
only a few tufts of down will show
through the growing feathers.

Eye shield — the eyebrow
that grows over the eye
socket, creating the
classic eagle scowl.

The beak develops a
hooked, sharp point.

The toes develop
long, hooked, sharp
claws called talons.

Day by day the nestlings grow bigger and stronger, but they still need the care and protection of their parents. One day a large dark bird flies too near the nest. It is a young eagle, a year or two old. The nestlings' mother and father scream and fly after the young eagle and chase it away.

PHASES: Age, Color, Pattern
(phases overlap and vary)

Fledgling, immature:
dark body, head, beak, and eye.

1-year.-old: breast bib, whitish
belly, lighter face and eye.

2-yr.-old: mottled belly, whiter
face, yellowish eye and beak.

3–4 yrs.: dark body, white face,
dark eye line, yellow beak and eye.

Adult, 4–5 yrs.: brown body and
wings, white head and tail, bright
yellow beak and yellow eye.

Seven weeks after hatching, the
nestlings have grown all their
feathers. Now they stand and stretch
their new feathers, feeling the air
currents rise around them.
One day the rising air lifts
one nestling . . . and then the other.

At 8 or 9 weeks the eaglets begin
branching (flapping and hopping
to branches of the nest tree) and
gliding to nearby trees. This helps
develop skills and strength, preparing
the young birds for real flight.

For several seconds they hang
in the air just above the nest —
their first small flight!
Every day after this the nestlings
face into the wind, stretch their
wings and tails, and flap their
wings, trying to fly.

11

Several weeks later, the mother and father eagles stop bringing food to the nestlings. It has been two or three days since they ate. They are very hungry. It is time for them to leave the nest. So the parents, carrying food in their talons, call to the nestlings from high in the sky. Excited by their calls and by the food they hold, one hungry nestling suddenly leaps from the edge of the nest. The other hesitates and then leaps into the air too.

At just ten weeks old, *they are flying!*

Awkwardly, the young eagles fly after their parents. One lands in a nearby tree. The father eagle brings it a fish. The other eaglet quickly returns to the nest. The mother eagle flies near the nest, showing it the fish she carries. Then, landing in another tree, she calls to the eaglet. Soon the hungry young bird flies to its mother and is rewarded with a fish. From now on, if the young eagles want to be fed, they will have to chase their parents.

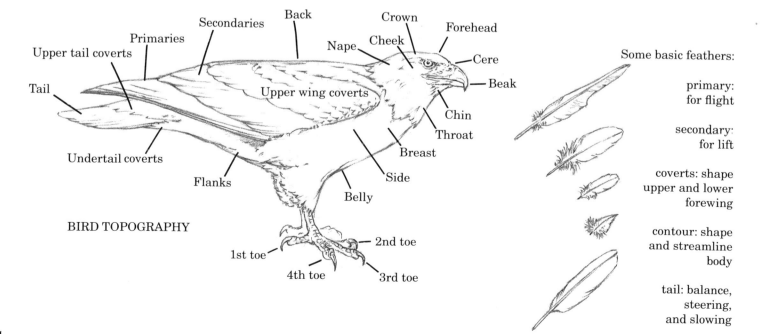

Secondaries
Back
Crown
Forehead
Primaries
Nape
Cheek
Upper tail coverts
Cere
Tail
Beak
Upper wing coverts
Chin
Throat
Undertail coverts
Breast
Flanks
Side
Belly
BIRD TOPOGRAPHY
2nd toe
1st toe
4th toe
3rd toe

Some basic feathers:

primary: for flight

secondary: for lift

coverts: shape upper and lower forewing

contour: shape and streamline body

tail: balance, steering, and slowing

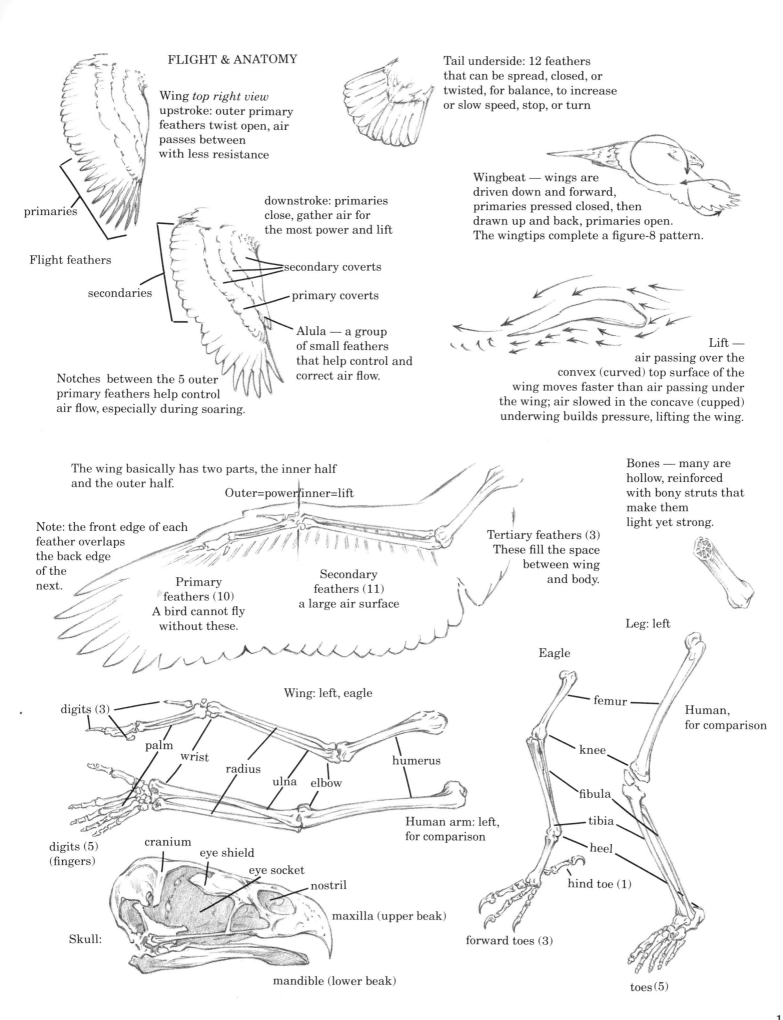

FLIGHT & ANATOMY

Wing *top right view*
upstroke: outer primary
feathers twist open, air
passes between
with less resistance

primaries

Flight feathers

secondaries

downstroke: primaries
close, gather air for
the most power and lift

secondary coverts

primary coverts

Alula — a group
of small feathers
that help control and
correct air flow.

Notches between the 5 outer
primary feathers help control
air flow, especially during soaring.

Tail underside: 12 feathers
that can be spread, closed, or
twisted, for balance, to increase
or slow speed, stop, or turn

Wingbeat — wings are
driven down and forward,
primaries pressed closed, then
drawn up and back, primaries open.
The wingtips complete a figure-8 pattern.

Lift —
air passing over the
convex (curved) top surface of the
wing moves faster than air passing under
the wing; air slowed in the concave (cupped)
underwing builds pressure, lifting the wing.

The wing basically has two parts, the inner half
and the outer half.

Outer=power/inner=lift

Note: the front edge of each
feather overlaps
the back edge
of the
next.

Primary
feathers (10)
A bird cannot fly
without these.

Secondary
feathers (11)
a large air surface

Tertiary feathers (3)
These fill the space
between wing
and body.

Bones — many are
hollow, reinforced
with bony struts that
make them
light yet strong.

Leg: left

Eagle

femur

Human,
for comparison

knee

fibula

tibia

heel

hind toe (1)

forward toes (3)

toes (5)

digits (3)

palm

wrist

radius

ulna

elbow

humerus

Wing: left, eagle

Human arm: left,
for comparison

digits (5)
(fingers)

cranium

eye shield

eye socket

nostril

maxilla (upper beak)

Skull:

mandible (lower beak)

Flying well takes strength and skill, and the young eagles need
lots of practice. But soon they are flying farther and higher,
leaving the nest and the valley far below.
They are no longer nestlings.

Watching the parents,
the young eagles learn how to
hunt for food. They
learn what they should catch and how to use
their strong feet and talons to keep what they catch.

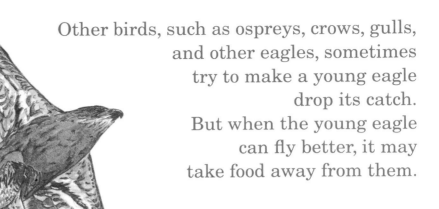

Other birds, such as ospreys, crows, gulls, and other eagles, sometimes try to make a young eagle drop its catch. But when the young eagle can fly better, it may take food away from them.

Hunting — An eagle catches prey with its powerful feet and sharp talons. Using its sharp, hooked beak, it plucks fur, feathers, or scales away from small areas of the body, then tears pieces of flesh away from the bones and tendons. Small prey may be swallowed whole.

Food includes rabbits, muskrats, and squirrels,

frogs, snakes, and turtles,

songbirds, ducks, seagulls, and shorebirds.

Eagles mostly eat fish.

Carrion (dead prey) is also a large part of an eagle's diet.

Pellet — a coughed-up lump of indigestible fur, feathers, scales, and bones.

"Fishing eagle" is another name for the bald eagle,
because these birds eat so much fish. But fish
are hard to catch, and sometimes an eagle
ends up in the water looking silly

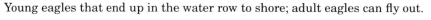

Doing it right — Spotting a fish at the water's surface, an eagle circles to size it up.
Dropping down, the bird makes a sharp corkscrew turn; then, spreading its wings
and tail to brake its speed, it brings its feet forward and snaps the fish from the water.
With a powerful downstroke the eagle lifts off with its catch.
Young eagles that end up in the water row to shore; adult eagles can fly out.

while the lucky fish escapes.

As winter comes the rivers and ponds begin to freeze.
Catching fish and hunting become difficult, so the
eagles leave the valley. They fly to a large
unfrozen river. Many eagles gather here.
It is a good place to fish and hunt during the winter months.

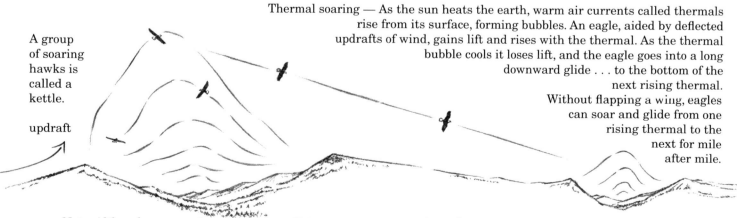

A group
of soaring
hawks is
called a
kettle.

updraft

Thermal soaring — As the sun heats the earth, warm air currents called thermals
rise from its surface, forming bubbles. An eagle, aided by deflected
updrafts of wind, gains lift and rises with the thermal. As the thermal
bubble cools it loses lift, and the eagle goes into a long
downward glide . . . to the bottom of the
next rising thermal.
Without flapping a wing, eagles
can soar and glide from one
rising thermal to the
next for mile
after mile.

Note: Although some eagles migrate long distances, most move only to the nearest open water,
returning to the same wintering area year after year.

In late winter or early spring the ice
melts on the rivers and ponds.
The adult male eagle returns to the nest area.
The nest was damaged by winter storms, so
he begins to repair it.

Eyrie — a remote nest site, usually
high in a treetop
or sometimes on a cliff ledge.

Nest — branches and twigs
lined with moss, grass, fresh
pine bough tips, and weeds.
5 feet across, 2 to 3 feet high.
Added to year after year;
sometimes reaches
7 to 8 feet across and 12 feet high.
Pairs mate for life. May
live 20 years in the wild.

A few days later the female
eagle returns. She calls to the male:
Chaeeeeeek-cheik-ik-ik-ik.
He recognizes her call and answers.
Together the eagles repair the nest,
adding sticks and making it
even bigger than it was before.
The young eagles they raised
last year do not return. They can fly
and hunt well enough to be
on their own.

Hawk family —
Eagles are members of the family Accipitridae.
All members of the hawk family are
predators with sharply hooked
beaks and long,
curved talons.

Eagles are the largest
hawks. There are
two native species, the
bald eagle and the
golden eagle.

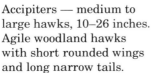

Bald Eagles —
34–44 inches long.
6 to 7½ foot wingspread.
male 8–10 lbs
female 10–14 lbs
Huge bird of
shorelines, with long
rounded wings and
broad rounded tails.

Accipiters — medium to
large hawks, 10–26 inches.
Agile woodland hawks
with short rounded wings
and long narrow tails.

Buteos — large stout
hawks up to 25 inches.
Soaring birds in
open country, with
broad wings and
wide rounded tails.

Harriers — only
North American harrier
is the northern harrier,
17–24 inches.
Slender bird of open
grassland or wetlands,
with long narrow
wings and tail.

Kites — medium hawks,
14–24 inches. Graceful
fliers of varying form,
usually having long
pointed wings and
long narrow tails.

25

Now the eagles start the courtship flight.
Flying high, they grab each other's feet and then fall,
tumbling and rolling out of the sky. Before they fall
too far they let go and soar again. Over and over they
chase, tumble, and roll out of the sky.

Courtship flight — The
male chases the
female high into the
sky. As he approaches
her from above or
from the side, she
reels, turns to face him,
and brings her
legs up. They lock their
feet together, then fall.
Cartwheeling, they drop
several hundred feet,
then let go and soar
skyward again. This
spectacular display
flight may occur only
occasionally during a
month or more of
frequent mating.

After the courtship flight, the male eagle
balances on the female's back with
his talons held in, and they mate.

After a month of mating
the female lays the first egg.
A day or two later she lays a second.
The male brings her food while she
incubates the eggs. He too will
take a turn sitting on the eggs
to keep them warm and dry.

Because incubation begins immediately with the
first egg laid (the second is laid within 36 hours),
all cycles between nestlings, from hatching
to fledging, usually occur several days apart.

When egg is laid, contents cool
and contract, forming air
space at the blunt end.

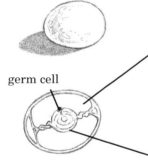

germ cell

Egg at time of laying:

albumen cushions
embryo and adds
nutriment

chalaza, a twisted
layer of albumen, holds
germ cell stationary
when egg is turned

yolk, the primary food supply

Developing embryo:

Allantois, or breathing
sac, passes gas (air)
between outside of
egg and embryo.
Also holds waste.

Fully developed embryo:

yolk sac is drawn into
the embryo just prior
to hatching, providing
the nestling with
basic nourishment.

Two days before hatching, the embryo breaks into the air
space and takes its first breath of air. It then starts
chirping and forcing its egg tooth against the inside of
the egg, eventually pipping or cracking it.
Laying to pipping takes approximately 35 days.
At this stage the hatching chick and female vocally communicate.

About thirty-five days later, the eagles
hear peeping sounds coming from
inside one of the eggs. A day or two
later peeping comes from
the second egg. It is now time for the
bald eagles to raise a new family.

Today a baby bird will hatch.